*s

Poems of Protest by William Morris

with an introduction by Michael Rosen &

afterword by Nicholas Salmon

Contents

Poems of Protest by William Morris
Introduction by Michael Rosen.
Afterword by Nicholas Salmon.
This collection published by Redwords 2013

ISBN: 978 1 909026 05 6

Design and production: Roger Huddle
Printed by The Russell Press, Nottingham

Redwords is linked to Bookmarks: the socialist bookshop
1 Bloomsbury Street London WC1B 3QE
redwords.org.uk
bookmarksbookshop.co.uk

Cover: Centre panel is Cray, a textile and wallpaer pattern
designed by William Morris in 1884, a year after he had
become a practical socialist, and his most complex design,
requiring 34 blocks for the hand printing.

Walter Crane for Commonweal

· LABOUR'S · MAY · DAY ·
DEDICATED · TO · THE · WORKERS · OF · THE · WORLD

Introduction: *Michael Rosen*

The place of Morris's political poetry

MY FATHER, Harold Rosen (1919-2009), was someone who often broke into song and I have memories of him singing two pieces that chime with this collection. To the tune of 'John Brown's Body' he would burst out with: 'What is this, the sound and rumour? What is this that all men hear, / Like the wind in hollow valleys when the storm is drawing near...' On other occasions he would sing something that sounded to me at the time like a lugubrious pirate song: 'Down, down, down, down/Down among the dead men let him lie!'

To set our compass right on these, I'm describing here scenes from the 1950s, either in a flat in London or on a camping holiday in Wales or Yorkshire, where a Jewish Communist brought up in London's East End, who picked up a raft of leftwing songs, particularly while at University College London in the late 1930s, was bringing to the surface that part of the repertoire of songs he held in his head which came from the socialist and revolutionary work of William Morris, and which in turn has survived in my head till now. It's a glimpse into how resistant culture and ideas are passed on.

Being a socialist, declaring that we believe in socialism, is locked into activism. We take part in campaigns, we do things in the now. This is only right but it can sometimes mean that we don't have time to look back over our shoulders to see what our socialist predecessors got up to. And we make choices about who we look back to, who we look up to. In an attempt to scoop together as many of these past defiant rebels as we could, David Widgery and I produced in 1991 *The Chatto Book of Dissent* (later *The Vintage Book of Dissent* in 1996) where we chose a passage taken from 'The Manifesto of the Socialist League' written in 1885 in which Morris talks of seeking 'a change in the basis of society — a change which would destroy the distinctions of classes and nationalities'.

Amidst the wallpapers and sofa coverings, it's easy to forget that Morris was an unequivocal revolutionary. It was the total transformation of society that he yearned and worked for. He was a prolific writer and speaker and, thanks largely to the work of Nicholas Salmon (1957-2002), a good deal of his words can be found online at *www.marxists. org/archive/morris/works/index.htm*, while many people will know of *Three Works*'(Lawrence and Wishart, 1968) which contains 'News from Nowhere', 'A Dream of John Ball' and 'The Pilgrims of Hope', the main works in which William Morris expressed in fictional form his socialist ideas.

So, William Morris's politics and ideas survive. But I'm not going to pretend it's easy keeping the words alive. As time passes, difficulties arise out of the context for the writing and the slow silt of condescension and contempt often falls very selectively on writers and poets whose works spread across the personal, fantastic and social over to the politically engaged. Within literary culture, there has arisen a snooty consensus that poetry and fiction should deal with the imagination, feelings, emotions and our personal interactions while politics, they say, should be left to politics. It's become a question of etiquette: serious newspapers produce thousands of words examining and praising the language and meaning of modern politicians' speeches but the moment such language is used or developed in poetry or fiction, a different set of criteria is brought out of the drawer. So, even as the poet and critic P J Kavanagh was praising Adrian Mitchell in 1996 for being a great 'performance poet', he felt it necessary to say of him: 'Of course he can be sentimental, of course his anarcho-pacifism can be used to rabble-rouse in too simple a way...' Meanwhile, at this very moment, some politician's speech-writer is desperately looking for what will in effect be a rhetoric as 'sentimental' and 'rabble-rousing' (in the terms of the snooty consensus) because that speech-writer knows that such language will be praised for stirring us on to greater things, showing us a vision, ringing true, engaging our sympathies...and all that. So, perhaps we can dispense with this inconsistency by saying that William Morris's socialist poetry is part of political rhetoric and part of how, through the way we speak and write, we have struggled for hundreds of years for a fair and just society.

The language of Morris's political poetry

Anyone coming to Morris's poetry for the first time is, I suspect, struck by the fact that it seems to be written in an antique voice. Take the first verse of the first poem in this collection and you find: 'Nor for my words shall ye forget your tears, / Or hope again for aught that I can say'. What has to be said is that it was antique in its own time. Most poets up until the last years of the nineteenth century felt that in order to be taken seriously, poetry needed to take on the clothes of a previous era, which in the English-speaking world was shot through with what was at the time the familiar and dominant voice of the King James Bible of 1611. Also descending from this source were the hymns, carols and prayers that millions of people knew off by heart. When we read or hear a Morris poem, we can get a sense of its context by imagining ourselves as capable of reciting, say, the first book of Genesis, and of singing the Psalms and maybe fifty hymns, prayers and carols.

Morris had a further reason to write like this: his thinking was much affected by an emotional and theoretical link to the medieval era. He used an idealised view of medieval life as a means by which to dissect and critique the degradation and inhumanity of contemporary life. In this he was part of the movement known as the Pre-Raphaelites. In most British city art galleries there are at least one or two paintings by this group. In these, you'll find religious, mythic or literary figures wearing ornate medieval clothes, often shown in rural settings and in some kind of tableau or symbolic pose. These may well appear to us as mystic and glorying in the authority and power of medieval Christian imagery and of the Church itself. Morris, though, was in effect an atheist, socialist Pre-Raphaelite. Perhaps we could say on his behalf that where his fellow pre-Raphaelites looked backwards in order to look backwards, Morris looked backwards in order to look forwards. For those unfamiliar with his work, this means that the imagery of his poetry – its pictures and scenes - are drawn from two main sources: a) the biblical and religious – so, we hear of 'reaping', 'sowing', 'gold', 'choirs', 'wise men' and 'slaves' while he talks of, say, 'knocking at the gate', 'the spire-top' or setting 'the crooked straight'; and b) the 'pastoral', that wellspring of language produced from Shakespeare's time onwards praising and adoring an idealised image of rural England: 'the happy fields we till', 'when men and maids are merry', 'Fair blossom the meadows for river to river' and so on.

So, a good deal of what Morris is doing in his socialist poetry is struggling against the ownership of this language and imagery, saying that this could and should belong to Socialists. Now, in the present day, this may seem a strange fight to pick, but he was grabbing the weapons being used by those wielding power in Victorian Britain and turning them against that same power. After all, this language and imagery had been used for hundreds of years as a way of telling working people that they had their place — as, famously, with:

All things bright and beautiful,
All creatures great and small,

All things wise and wonderful,
The Lord God made them all.

Each little flower that opens,
Each little bird that sings,
He made their glowing colours,
He made their tiny wings.

All things bright and beautiful,
All creatures great and small,
All things wise and wonderful
The Lord God made them all.

The rich man in his castle,
The poor man at his gate,
God made them high and lowly,
And ordered their estate.

More often than not, the poetry of protest in the modern era has tried to avoid the language of the powerful in order to fight back against the powerful. Langston Hughes, for example, developed the speech of contemporary working class African Americans and the details of their everday life as the means by which to assault those in power. For Morris, it's clear that the array of medieval, rural and religious symbols seemed the most potent and populist imagery to use for similar purposes.

One thought to add here: if we talk of symbols, we are talking of a consciously crafted double language. So when Morris talks of, say, 'hovels', this is of course a rural image, laden with ideas of earth floors, people sleeping alongside animals, broken thatched roofs and the like, but he is at the same time referring to the terraced houses in the back streets of Manchester, Newcastle, Birmingham and London. When he talks of workers reaping half for nothing 'by him that sowed the seed', he is at one level showing us rural work, but through that image he is talking about industrial workers producing what Marx called 'surplus value'. This was a political tactic usedby Morris and he knew that this was the kind of language and ideas that almost all of his audience would have been familiar with. It was revolutionary to use it in the way that he did.

Note on the collection   The poems in this book are arranged in the order in which they were written (as far as is known) and have never been assembled in this way before. Morris's socialist poems were collected by him and published many times under the title of *Chants for Socialists* (1885) and all these appear in this volume in the full expanded edition of ten poems as published by Longmans, Green and Company in 1915. However, I've added to these three others: one poem, (The Earthly Paradise: Apology), from the huge collection of his poetry not usually regarded as explicitly political; the first overtly and deliberately political poem that Morris wrote (Wake London Lads); and a poem that Morris wrote for his fellow political activists, (Socialists at Play), giving us 13 poems in all. I should add here that the last of the *Chants for Socialists,* (The Message of the March Wind) is the first poem of Morris's experimental political verse novel, *The Pilgrims of Hope* which you can find online and in *Three Works by William Morris*, the Lawrence and Wishart volume I have already mentioned.

Edward Burne-Jones

The Earthly Paradise: Apology

from the
Prologue 1868

Of Heaven or Hell I have no power to sing,
I cannot ease the burden of your fears,
Or make quick-coming death a little thing,
Or bring again the pleasure of past years,
Nor for my words shall ye forget your tears,
Or hope again for aught that I can say,
The idle singer of an empty day.

But rather, when aweary of your mirth,
From full hearts still unsatisfied ye sigh,
And, feeling kindly unto all the earth,
Grudge every minute as it passes by,
Made the more mindful that the sweet days die—
Remember me a little then I pray,
The idle singer of an empty day.

The heavy trouble, the bewildering care
That weighs us down who live and earn our bread,
These idle verses have no power to bear;
So let me sing of names remembered,
Because they, living not, can ne'er be dead,
Or long time take their memory quite away
From us poor singers of an empty day.

Dreamer of dreams, born out of my due time,
Why should I strive to set the crooked straight?
Let it suffice me that my murmuring rhyme
Beats with light wing against the ivory gate,
Telling a tale not too importunate
To those who in the sleepy region stay,
Lulled by the singer of an empty day.

The Earthly
Paradise:
Apology

Folk say, a wizard to a northern king
At Christmas-tide such wondrous things did show,
That through one window men beheld the spring,
And through another saw the summer glow,
And through a third the fruited vines a-row,
While still, unheard, but in its wonted way,
Piped the drear wind of that December day.

So with this Earthly Paradise it is,
If ye will read aright, and pardon me,
Who strive to build a shadowy isle of bliss
Midmost the beating of the steely sea,
Where tossed about all hearts of men must be;
Whose ravening monsters mighty men shall slay,
Not the poor singer of an empty day.

Wake, London Lads

Wake, London Lads, wake, bold and free!
    Arise, and fall to work,
Lest England's glory come to be
    Bond servant to the Turk!
Think of your Sires! how oft and oft
    On freedom's field they bled,
When Cromwell's hand was raised aloft,
    And Kings and scoundrels fled.

From out the dusk, from out the dark,
    Of old our fathers came,
Till lovely freedom's glimmering spark
    Broke forth a glorious flame:
And shall we now praise freedom's dearth
    And rob the years to come
And quench upon a brother's hearth
    The fires we lit at home?

O, happy England, if thine hand
    Should forge anew the chain,
The fetters of a tortured land,
    How were thy glory vain!
Our serving men, our women's tears,
    The graves of those we love,
Should buy us curses for all years,
    A weight we might not move.

Yea, through the fog of unjust war
    What thief on us might steal,
To rob us of the gifts of yore,
    The hope of England's weal?
The toilsome years have built and earned,

Wake,
London
Lads

Great men in hope have died;
Shall all the lesson be unlearned,
    The treasure scattered wide?

What! shall we crouch beneath the load,
    And call the labour sweet,
And, dumb and blind, go down the road
    Where shame abides our feet?
Wake, London Lads! the hour draws nigh,
    The bright sun brings the day;
Cast off the shame, cast off the lie,
    And cast the Turk away!

Chants for Socialists

Banner by Walter Crane

The Day is Coming

Come hither, lads, and hearken, for a tale there is
    to tell,
Of the wonderful days a-coming, when all shall be
    better than well.

And the tale shall be told of a country, a land in the
    midst of the sea,
And folk shall call it England in the days that are
    going to be.

There more than one in a thousand in the days that
    are yet to come
Shall have some hope of the morrow, some joy of
    the ancient home.

For then – laugh not, but listen to this strange tale
    of mine –
All folk that are in England shall be better lodged
    than swine.

Then a man shall work and bethink him, and
    rejoice in the deeds of his hand,
Nor yet come home in the even too faint and weary
    to stand.

Men in that time a-coming shall work and have no
    fear
For to-morrow's lack of earning and the hunger-
    wolf anear.

I tell you this for a wonder, that no man then shall
    be glad

Of his fellow's fall and mishap to snatch at the
work he had.

For that which the worker winneth shall then be
his indeed,
Nor shall half be reaped for nothing by him that
sowed no seed.

O strange new wonderful justice! But for whom
shall we gather the gain? For ourselves and for
each of our fellows, and no
hand shall labour in vain.

Then all Mine and all Thine shall be Ours, and no
more shall any man crave
For riches that serve for nothing but to fetter a
friend for a slave.

And what wealth then shall be left us when none
shall gather gold
To buy his friend in the market, and pinch and pine
the sold?

Nay, what save the lovely city, and the little house
on the hill,
And the wastes and the woodland beauty, and the
happy fields we till;

And the homes of ancient stories, the tombs of the
mighty dead;
And the wise men seeking out marvels, and the
poet's teeming head;

And the painter's hand of wonder; and the
    marvellous fiddle-bow,
And the banded choirs of music: all those that do
    and know.

For all these shall be ours and all men's, nor shall
    any lack a share
Of the toil and the gain of living in the days when
    the world grows fair.

Ah! such are the days that shall be! But what are
    the deeds of to-day,
In the days of the years we dwell in, that wear our
    lives away?

Why, then, and for what are we waiting? There are
    three words to speak:
We will it, and what is the foeman but the
    dream-strong wakened and weak?

O why and for what are we waiting? While our
    brothers droop and die,
And on every wind of the heavens a wasted life
    goes by.

How long shall they reproach us where crowd on
    crowd they dwell,
Poor ghosts of the wicked city, the gold-crushed
    hungry hell?

Through squalid life they laboured, in sordid grief
    they died,
Those sons of a mighty mother, those props of
    England's pride.

They are gone; there is none can undo it, nor save
    our souls from the curse;
But many a million cometh, and shall they be
    better or worse?

It is we must answer and hasten, and open wide
    the door
For the rich man's hurrying terror, and the slow-
    foot hope of the poor.

Yea, the voiceless wrath of the wretched, and their
    unlearned discontent,
We must give it voice and wisdom till the waiting-
    tide be spent.

Come, then, since all things call us, the living and
    the dead,
And o'er the weltering tangle a glimmering light is
    shed.

Come, then, let us cast off fooling, and put by ease
    and rest,
For the CAUSE alone is worthy till the good days
    bring the best.

Come, join in the only battle wherein no man can
    fail,
Where whoso fadeth and dieth, yet his deed shall
    still prevail.

Ah! come, cast off all fooling, for this, at least, we
    know:
That the Dawn and the Day is coming, and forth
    the Banners go.

The Voice of Toil

I heard men saying, Leave hope and praying,
All days shall be as all have been;
To-day and to-morrow bring fear and sorrow,
The never-ending toil between.

When Earth was younger mid toil and hunger,
In hope we strove, and our hands were strong;
Then great men led us, with words they fed us,
And bade us right the earthly wrong.

Go read in story their deeds and glory,
Their names amidst the nameless dead;
Turn then from lying to us slow-dying
In that good world to which they led;

Where fast and faster our iron master,
The thing we made, for ever drives,
Bids us grind treasure and fashion pleasure
For other hopes and other lives.

Where home is a hovel and dull we grovel,
Forgetting that the world is fair;
Where no babe we cherish, lest its very soul perish;
Where our mirth is crime, our love a snare.

Who now shall lead us, what god shall heed us
As we lie in the hell our hands have won?
For us are no rulers but fools and befoolers,
The great are fallen, the wise men gone.

I heard men saying, Leave tears and praying,
The sharp knife heedeth not the sheep;

Are we not stronger than the rich and the wronger,
When day breaks over dreams and sleep?

Come, shoulder to shoulder ere the world grows older!
Help lies in nought but thee and me;
Hope is before us, the long years that bore us
Bore leaders more than men may be.

Let dead hearts tarry and trade and marry,
And trembling nurse their dreams of mirth,
While we the living our lives are giving
To bring the bright new world to birth.

Come, shoulder to shoulder ere earth grows older
The Cause spreads over land and sea;
Now the world shaketh, and fear awaketh
And joy at last for thee and me.

All for the Cause

Hear a word, a word in season, for the day is
  drawing nigh,
When the Cause shall call upon us, some to live,
  and some to die!

He that dies shall not die lonely, many an one hath
  gone before;
He that lives shall bear no burden heavier than the
  life they bore.

Nothing ancient is their story, e'en but yesterday
  they bled,
Youngest they of earth's beloved, last of all the
  valiant dead.

E'en the tidings we are telling was the tale they had
  to tell,
E'en the hope that our hearts cherish, was the hope
  for which they fell.

In the grave where tyrants thrust them, lies their
  labour and their pain,
But undying from their sorrow springeth up the
  hope again.

Mourn not therefore, nor lament it, that the world
  outlives their life;
Voice and vision yet they give us, making strong our
  hands for strife.

Some had name, and fame, and honour, learn'd they
  were, and wise and strong;

Some were nameless, poor, unlettered, weak in all
    but grief and wrong.

Named and nameless all live in us; one and all they
    lead us yet
Every pain to count for nothing, every sorrow to
    forget.

Hearken how they cry, "O happy, happy ye that ye
    were born
In the sad slow night's departing, in the rising of the
    morn.

"Fair the crown the Cause hath for you, well to die
    or well to live
Through the battle, through the tangle, peace to gain
    or peace to give."

Ah, it may be! Oft meseemeth, in the days that yet
    shall be,
When no slave of gold abideth 'twixt the breadth of
    sea to sea,

Oft, when men and maids are merry, ere the sunlight
    leaves the earth,
And they bless the day beloved, all too short for all
    their mirth,

Some shall pause awhile and ponder on the bitter
    days of old,
Ere the toil of strife and battle overthrew the curse
    of gold;

Then 'twixt lips of loved and lover solemn thoughts
of us shall rise;
We who once were fools and dreamers, then shall
be the brave and wise.

There amidst the world new-builded shall our
earthly deeds abide,
Though our names be all forgotten, and the tale of
how we died.

Life or death then, who shall heed it, what we gain
or what we lose?
Fair flies life amid the struggle, and the Cause for
each shall choose.

Hear a word, a word in season, for the day is
drawing nigh,
When the Cause shall call upon us, some to live,
and some to die!

No Master

Saith man to man, We've heard and known
That we no master need
To live upon this earth, our own,
In fair and manly deed.
The grief of slaves long passed away
For us hath forged the chain,
Till now each worker's patient day
Builds up the House of Pain.

And we, shall we too, crouch and quail,
Ashamed, afraid of strife,
And lest our lives untimely fail
Embrace the Death in Life?
Nay, cry aloud, and have no fear,
We few against the world;
Awake, arise! the hope we bear
Against the curse is hurled.

It grows and grows – are we the same,
The feeble band, the few?
Or what are these with eyes aflame,
And hands to deal and do?
This is the host that bears the word,
No Master high or low –
A lightning flame, a shearing sword,
A storm to overthrow.

The March of the Workers

What is this, the sound and rumour? What is this
    that all men hear,
Like the wind in hollow valleys when the storm is
    drawing near,
Like the rolling on of ocean in the eventide of fear?
'Tis the people marching on.

Whither go they, and whence come they? What are
    these of whom ye tell?
In what country are they dwelling 'twixt the gates
    of heaven and hell?
Are they mine or thine for money? Will they serve
    a master well?
Still the rumour's marching on.

    Hark the rolling of the thunder!
    Lo the sun! and lo thereunder
    Riseth wrath, and hope, and wonder,
    And the host comes marching on.

Forth they come from grief and torment; on they
    wend toward health and mirth,
All the wide world is their dwelling, every corner
    of the earth.
Buy them, sell them for thy service! Try the
    bargain what 'tis worth,
For the days are marching on.

These are they who build thy houses, weave thy
    raiment, win thy wheat,
Smooth the rugged, fill the barren, turn the bitter
    into sweet,

35

All for thee this day — and ever. What reward for
    them is meet
Till the host comes marching on?

    Hark the rolling of the thunder!
    Lo the sun! and lo thereunder
    Riseth wrath, and hope, and wonder,
    And the host comes marching on.

Many a hundred years passed over have they
    laboured deaf and blind;
Never tidings reached their sorrow, never hope
    their toil might find.
Now at last they've heard and hear it, and the cry
    comes down the wind,
And their feet are marching on.

O ye rich men hear and tremble! for with words
    the sound is rife:
"Once for you and death we laboured; changed
    henceforward is the strife.
We are men, and we shall battle for the world of
    men and life;
And our host is marching on."

    Hark the rolling of the thunder!
    Lo the sun! and lo thereunder
    Riseth wrath, and hope, and wonder,
    And the host comes marching on.

"Is it war, then? Will ye perish as the dry wood in
    the fire?
Is it peace? Then be ye of us, let your hope be our
    desire.

Come and live! for life awaketh, and the world
   shall never tire;
And hope is marching on.

"On we march then, we the workers, and the
   rumour that ye hear
Is the blended sound of battle and deliv'rance
   drawing near;
For the hope of every creature is the banner that
   we bear,
And the world is marching on."

   Hark the rolling of the thunder!
   Lo the sun! and lo thereunder
   Riseth wrath, and hope, and wonder,
   And the host comes marching on.

The Message of the March Wind

Fair now is the springtide, now earth lies beholding
With the eyes of a lover the face of the sun;
Long lasteth the daylight, and hope is enfolding
The green-growing acres with increase begun.

Now sweet, sweet it is through the land to be straying
Mid the birds and the blossoms and the beasts of the field;
Love mingles with love, and no evil is weighing
On thy heart or mine, where all sorrow is healed.

From township to township, o'er down and by tillage
Far, far have we wandered and long was the day,
But now cometh eve at the end of the village,
Where over the grey wall the church riseth grey.

There is wind in the twilight; in the white road before us
The straw from the ox-yard is blowing about;
The moon's rim is rising, a star glitters o'er us,
And the vane on the spire-top is swinging in doubt.

Down there dips the highway, toward the bridge crossing
    over
The brook that runs on to the Thames and the sea.
Draw closer, my sweet, we are lover and lover;
This eve art thou given to gladness and me.

Shall we be glad always? Come closer and hearken:
Three fields further on, as they told me down there,
When the young moon has set, if the March sky should
    darken,
We might see from the hill-top the great city's glare.

38

Hark, the wind in the elm-boughs! From London it
    bloweth,
And telling of gold, and of hope and unrest;
Of power that helps not; of wisdom that knoweth,
But teacheth not aught of the worst and the best.

Of the rich men it telleth, and strange is the story
How they have, and they hanker, and grip far and wide;
And they live and they die, and the earth and its glory
Has been but a burden they scarce might abide.

Hark! the March wind again of a people is telling;
Of the life that they live there, so haggard and grim,
That if we and our love amidst them had been dwelling
My fondness had faltered, thy beauty grown dim.

This land we have loved in our love and our leisure
For them hangs in heaven, high out of their reach;
The wide hills o'er the sea-plain for them have no
    pleasure,
The grey homes of their fathers no story to teach.

The singers have sung and the builders have builded,
The painters have fashioned their tales of delight;
For what and for whom hath the world's book been
    gilded,
When all is for these but the blackness of night?

How long and for what is their patience abiding?
How oft and how oft shall their story be told,
While the hope that none seeketh in darkness is hiding
And in grief and in sorrow the world groweth old?

Come back to the inn, love, and the lights and the fire,
And the fiddler's old tune and the shuffling of feet;
For there in a while shall be rest and desire,
And there shall the morrow's uprising be sweet.

Yet, love, as we wend the wind bloweth behind us
And beareth the last tale it telleth to-night,
How here in the spring-tide the message shall find us;
For the hope that none seeketh is coming to light.

Like the seed of midwinter, unheeded, unperished,
Like the autumn-sown wheat 'neath the snow lying green,
Like the love that o'ertook us, unawares and uncherished,
Like the babe 'neath thy girdle that groweth unseen,

So the hope of the people now buddeth and groweth —
Rest fadeth before it, and blindness and fear;
It biddeth us learn all the wisdom it knoweth;
It hath found us and held us, and biddeth us hear:

For it beareth the message: "Rise up on the morrow
And go on your ways toward the doubt and the strife;
Join hope to our hope and blend sorrow with sorrow,
And seek for men's love in the short days of life."

But lo, the old inn, and the lights and the fire,
And the fiddler's old tune and the shuffling of feet;
Soon for us shall be quiet and rest and desire,
And to-morrow's uprising to deeds shall be sweet.

Down Among the Dead Men

Come, comrades, come, your glasses clink;
Up with your hands a health to drink,
The health of all that workers be,
In every land, on every sea.
And he that will this health deny,
Down among the dead men, down among the dead men,
Down, down, down, down,
Down among the dead men let him lie!

Well done! now drink another toast,
And pledge the gath'ring of the host,
The people armed in brain and hand,
To claim their rights in every land.
And he that will this health deny,
Down among the dead men, down among the dead men,
Down, down, down, down,
Down among the dead men let him lie!

There's liquor left; come, let's be kind,
And drink the rich a better mind,
That when we knock upon the door,
They may be off and say no more.
And he that will this health deny,
Down among the dead men, down among the dead men,
Down, down, down, down,
Down among the dead men let him lie!

Now, comrades, let the glass blush red,
Drink we the unforgotten dead
That did their deeds and went away,
Before the bright sun brought the day.
And he that will this health deny,

Down among the dead men, down among the dead men,
Down, down, down, down,
Down among the dead men let him lie!

The Day? Ah, friends, late grows the night;
Drink to the glimmering spark of light,
The herald of the joy to be,
The battle-torch of thee and me!
And he that will this health deny,
Down among the dead men, down among the dead men,
Down, down, down, down,
Down among the dead men let him lie!

Take yet another cup in hand
And drink in hope our little band;
Drink strife in hope while lasteth breath,
And brotherhood in life and death;
And he that will this health deny,
Down among the dead men, down among the dead men,
Down, down, down, down,
Down among the dead men let him lie!

Socialists at Play

Friends, we have met amidst our busy life
To rest an hour from turmoil and from strife,
To cast our care aside while song and verse
Touches our hearts, and lulls the ancient curse.
And yet — what's this? To no luxurious mood
By what we hear tonight shall be wooed.
War, labour, freedom; noble words are these;
But must we hymn them in our hours of ease? —
We must be men. You comrades, you who came
In trust of England's ancient honoured name
Unto this 'home of freedom o'er the wave.'
'This loosener of the fetters of the slave,'
E'en here have felt the petty tyrant's will,
Who robs and worries where he may not kill.
We must be men, or we shall find one day
Our boasted safe asylum swept away:
The blue-coat's staff, the spy's report, shall be
Emblems of England's saved society.

Yet more, what's this? The wail shall reach our ears
Wherewith Hood moved the listening town to tears —
But not to deeds: and your familiar friend
Shall bear his rough rhymes with your longings blend,
Ashamed to think how little he may do
To share his lot with labour and with you.
Lastly, we pray you ere we part to raise
Your voices once more in the 'Marseillaise,'
The glorious strain that long ago foretold
The hope now multiplied a thousand fold:
Nay, hope transfigured; since at last we know
The world our country, and the rich our foe.

So through our play, as in our work, we see
The strife that is, the Peace that is to be.
We are as warriors waiting for the word
That breaks the truce and calls upon the sword:
Gay is their life and merry men they are,
But all about then savours of the war.
Their glittering arms are all their childrens' toys,
Amidst their ballad sings the trumpet's voice;
About the sheep-cotes girt for war they go,
Pale gleams the glaive above the seed they sow.

All this is good; let other men forget!
Let others rest while they are living yet!
But we, but we — what time have we for rest,
Who see the worst, who see the coming best?
Long is our task, and soon the day is o'er,
And once departed cometh back no more.
How good the stroke once struck! How good the deed
Done once for all! How good the help at need!

So be we gay; but yet, amidst our mirth,
Remember how the sorrow of the earth
Has called upon us till we hear and know
And save as dastards never back may go!
Why, then, should we forget? Let the cause cling
About the book we read, the song we sing,
Cleave to our cup and hover o'er our plate,
And by our bed at morn and even wait.
Let the sun shine upon it; let the night
Weave happy tales of our fulfilled delight!
The child we cherish and the love we love,
Let these our hearts to deeper daring move:
Let deedful life be sweet and death no dread,
For us, the last men risen from the dead!

Thus shall we barter what poor ease and rest
Is yet our own amidst a world oppressed
For deeds and hope of deeds: thus shall we see
Clear if far off better days to be;
And live like men nor lack for helpful friends
Whatever fate the time upon us sends.

There! let the peddling world go staggering by
Propped up by lies and vain hypocrisy,
While here we stand amidst the scorn and hate,
Crying aloud the certain tale of fate,
Bidding the happy day when sword, in hand
Shall greet the sun and bless the tortured land.

Walter Crane

A Death Song

What cometh here from west to east awending?
And who are these, the marchers stern and slow?
We bear the message that the rich are sending
Aback to those who bade them wake and know.
Not one, not one, nor thousands must they slay,
But one and all if they would dusk the day.

We asked them for a life of toilsome earning,
They bade us bide their leisure for our bread;
We craved to speak to tell our woeful learning:
We come back speechless, bearing back our dead.
Not one, not one, nor thousands must they slay,
But one and all if they would dusk the day.

They will not learn; they have no ears to hearken.
They turn their faces from the eyes of fate;
Their gay-lit halls shut out the skies that darken.
But, lo! this dead man knocking at the gate.
Not one, not one, nor thousands must they slay,
But one and all if they would dusk the day.

Here lies the sign that we shall break our prison;
Amidst the storm he won a prisoner's rest;
But in the cloudy dawn the sun arisen
Brings us our day of work to win the best.
Not one, not one, nor thousands must they slay,
But one and all if they would dusk the day.

May Day [1892]

THE WORKERS
O Earth, once again cometh Spring to deliver
Thy winter-worn heart, O thou friend of the Sun;
Fair blossom the meadows from river to river
And the birds sing their triumph o'er winter undone.

O Earth, how a-toiling thou singest thy labour
And upholdest the flower-crowned cup of thy bliss,
As when in the feast-tide drinks neighbour to neighbour
And all words are gleeful, and nought is amiss.

But we, we, O Mother, through long generations,
We have toiled and been fruitful, but never with thee
Might we raise up our bowed heads and cry to the nations
To look on our beauty, and hearken our glee.

Unlovely of aspect, heart-sick and a-weary
On the season's fair pageant all dim-eyed we gaze;
Of thy fairness we fashion a prison-house dreary
And in sorrow wear over each day of our days.

THE EARTH.
O children! O toilers, what foemen beleaguer
The House I have built you, the Home I have won?
Full great are my gifts, and my hands are all eager
To fill every heart with the deeds I have done.

THE WORKERS.
The foemen are born of thy body, O Mother,
In our shape are they shapen, their voice is the same;
And the thought of their hearts is as ours and no other;
It is they of our own house that bring us to shame.

48

THE EARTH.
Are ye few? Are they many? What words have ye
spoken
To bid your own brethren remember the Earth?
What deeds have ye done that the bonds should be
broken,
And men dwell together in good-will and mirth?

THE WORKERS.
They are few, we are many: and yet, O our Mother,
Many years were we wordless and nought was our
deed,
But now the word flitteth from brother to brother:
We have furrowed the acres and scattered the seed.

THE EARTH.
Win on then unyielding, through fair and foul weather,
And pass not a day that your deed shall avail.
And in hope every spring-tide come gather together
That unto the Earth ye may tell all your tale.

Then this shall I promise, that I am abiding
The day of your triumph, the ending of gloom,
And no wealth that ye will then my hand shall be hiding
And the tears of the spring into roses shall bloom.

· A · GARLAND · FOR · MAY · DAY · 1895 ·
· DEDICATED · TO · THE · WORKERS · BY · WALTER · CRANE ·

May Day, 1894

Clad is the year in all her best,
The land is sweet and sheen;
Now Spring with Summer at her breast,
Goes down the meadows green.

Here are we met to welcome in
The young abounding year,
To praise what she would have us win
Ere winter draweth near.

For surely all is not in vain,
This gallant show she brings;
But seal of hope and sign of gain,
Beareth this Spring of springs.

No longer now the seasons wear
Dull, without any tale
Of how the chain the toilers bear
Is growing thin and frail.

But hope of plenty and goodwill
Flies forth from land to land,
Nor any now the voice can still
That crieth on the hand.

A little while shall Spring come back
And find the Ancient Home
Yet marred by foolish waste and lack,
And most enthralled by some.

A little while, and then at last
Shall the greetings of the year

Be blent with wonder of the past
And all the griefs that were.

A little while, and they that meet
The living year to praise,
Shall be to them as music sweet
That grief of bye-gone days.

So be we merry to our best,
Now the land is sweet and sheen,
And Spring with Summer at her breast
Goes down the meadows green.

'THE EARTHLY PARADISE: APOLOGY'
The Earthly Paradise is a four part epic poem, first
published in three volumes between 1868 and 1870. It
owes a lot to Chaucer's *The Canterbury Tales*, telling the
story of a group of Norsemen, fleeing the Black Death,
who come upon an unknown island in the Adriatic
peopled by descendants of the ancient Greeks. The
wanderers and the inhabitants of the island agree to tell
each other tales from their respective heritages, one from
each side each month between March and December. It
is then what's known as a 'frame story' with a narrator
giving the story of the people doing the story-telling. This
narrator is the person who recites the 'Apology' which I
have selected here, but who also narrates lyric poems in
between the tales and an Epilogue to the whole poem. I
chose to include this poem in the collection because it is
a fairly undisguised statement of atheism or 'unbelief', a
rare and subversive idea in Victorian England.

'WAKE, LONDON LADS'
This was written in January 1878 and was intended to
be sung to the tune of 'The Hardy Norseman's Home of
Yore'.
It is the first of Morris's poems written for explicitly
propaganda purposes, by way of an introduction
to a meeting on 16 January 1878, in Exeter Hall in
the Strand, London, where the Strand Palace Hotel
stands today. The meeting was called to protest against
England being dragged into a war. 'Wake, London Lads'
was sung by a choir at the beginning of the meeting
who, as Morris wrote in a letter, 'struck up while we
were just ready to come on to the platform and you can

53

imagine I felt rather excited when I heard them begin
to tune up: they stopped at the end of each verse and
cheered lustily: we came on to the platform just about
the middle of it.'

The politics the song addressed are that Britain was on
the verge of participating in an 'unjust war' on behalf
of the 'Turks' and that such an intervention would, he
and the left of the time thought, endanger the tradition
of liberty. By 1880, Morris was writing and talking of
the horrors of war, the injustice it produces even as it
talks of the interests of the country, as in his speech 'Our
Country Right or Wrong'.

'THE DAY IS COMING'
First published in February 1883.
It was probably the success of 'Wake, London Lads'
which encouraged Morris to write more songs for the
socialist cause. As he wrote in *Commonweal*, the paper
of the Socialist League in April 1885, 'a cause which
cannot be sung of is not worth following'. The first
group of these songs was begun in 1884 when this poem
appeared in the socialist paper *Justice* on 29 March and
included in a pamphlet published by the Marxist group
the Social Democratic Federation.

'THE VOICE OF TOIL'
Published in *Justice* on April 5, 1884.

'ALL FOR THE CAUSE'
Published in *Justice* on April 19, 1884

'NO MASTER
Published in *Justice* on 7 June 1884; sung to the tune of
'The Hardy Norseman's Home of Yore'.

'THE MARCH OF THE WORKERS'
Published in *Commonweal* in February 1885; sung to
the tune of 'John Brown's Body' and a rewrite of the
'Battle Hymn of the Republic'.

'THE MESSAGE OF THE MARCH WIND'
Published in *Commonweal* in March 1885 and is the
first of the 13 poems which make up 'The Pilgrims of
Hope' — a socialist verse novel depicting the struggle
of three modern people to survive their own personal
problems whilst committing to the socialist cause.

[Please note: poems 3 to 8 were published by the
Socialist League as *Chants for Socialists* in 1885]

'DOWN AMONG THE DEAD MEN'
Published first in a later edition of *Chants for Socialists*.
It is a parody of:
words John Dyer (1700-58); music traditional

Here's a health to the Queen and a lasting peace,
To faction an end, to wealth increase;
Come, let us drink it while we have breath,
For there's no drinking after death,
And he that will this health deny,

Down among the dead men,
Down among the dead men,
Down, down, down, down,
Down among the dead men let him lie.

Let charming Beauty's health go round,
In whom celestial joys are found;
And may confusion still pursue,

The senseless woman hating crew,
And they that woman's health deny;

May love and wine their joys maintain,
And their united pleasures reign;
While smiling plenty crowns the land,
We'll sing the joys that both afford:
And they that won't with us comply.

[*nb* the 'dead men' in this drinking song are empty
bottles!]

'SOCIALISTS AT PLAY'
Published in *Commonweal* in 1885 and also as a
pamphlet published by the Socialist League.

'A DEATH SONG'
Published as a penny pamphlet as a memorial to Alfred
Linnell who died as a result of injuries he received in
Trafalgar Square on Bloody Sunday, 1887.
This poem was added to *Chants for Socialists* in later
editions. It was originally produced for Linnell's funeral
on 18 November and the pamphlet carried
an illustration by Walter Crane depicting a policeman
clubbing Linnell. All proceeds of the pamphlet were
donated to a fund for the benefit of Linnell's orphans.

'MAY DAY'
First published in 1892.

'MAY DAY'
First published in 1894.

For some of the above information, I am indebted to the late Nicholas Salmon and his scholarly essay, The Communist Poet-Laureate: William Morris's Chants for Socialists — see afterword in this edition page 67

Notes on the poems

SEE ALSO:
Christopher Waters: 'Morris's "Chants" and the Problems of Socialist Culture' in *Socialism and the Literary Artistry of William Morris* edited by Florence S. Boos and Carole G. Silver (University of Missouri Press, Columbia and London, 1990) and available here: *http://morrisedition.lib.uiowa.edu/WatersPW.pdf*

'William Morris's Chants for Socialists and the Problem of Utopia' (May 2012) by Fabian Macpherson to be found here: *http://www.bbk.ac.uk/cprc/events/Fabian_McPherson_-_Poetry_and_Revolution_conference_paper.pdf*

Morris with members of the Hammersmith branch of the Socialist League, 1885. His daughter May is in the centre and the architect Philip Webb stands on the far left holding his bowler hat. Morris is on the right of the middle row with his arm across his chest and a full grey beard.

58

William Morris
How I Became a Socialist

First published
in *Justice*,
16 June 1894

I AM ASKED BY THE EDITOR to give some sort of a history of the above conversion, and I feel that it may be of some use to do so, if my readers will look upon me as a type of a certain group of people, but not so easy to do clearly, briefly and truly. Let me, however, try. But first, I will say what I mean by being a Socialist, since I am told that the word no longer expresses definitely and with certainty what it did ten years ago. Well, what I mean by Socialism is a condition of society in which there should be neither rich nor poor, neither master nor master's man, neither idle nor overworked, neither brain-sick brain workers, nor heart-sick hand workers, in a word, in which all men would be living in equality of condition, and would manage their affairs unwastefully, and with the full consciousness that harm to one would mean harm to all—the realization at last of the meaning of the word COMMONWEALTH.

Now this view of Socialism which I hold to-day, and hope to die holding, is what I began with; I had no transitional period, unless you may call such a brief period of political radicalism during which I saw my ideal clear enough, but had no hope of any realization of it. That came to an end some months before I joined the (then) Democratic Federation, and the meaning of my joining that body was that I had conceived a hope of the realization of my ideal. If you ask me how much of a hope, or what I thought we Socialists then living and working would accomplish towards it, or when there would be effected any change in the face of society, I must say, I do not know. I can only say that I did not measure my hope, nor the joy that it brought me at the time. For the rest, when I took that step I was blankly ignorant of economics; I had never so much as opened Adam Smith, or heard of Ricardo, or of Karl Marx. Oddly enough, I had read some of Mill, to wit, those posthumous papers of his (published, was it in the Westminster Review or the Fortnightly?) in which he attacks Socialism in its Fourierist guise. In those papers he put the arguments, as far as they go, clearly and honestly, and the result, so far as I was concerned, was to convince me that Socialism was a necessary change, and that it was possible to bring it about in our own days. Those papers put the finishing touch to my conversion to Socialism. Well, having joined a Socialist body (for the Federation soon became definitely Socialist), I put some conscience into trying to learn the economical side of Socialism, and even tackled Marx, though I must confess that, whereas I thoroughly enjoyed the historical part of Capital, I suffered agonies of confusion of the brain over reading the pure economics of that great work. Anyhow, I read what I could, and will hope that some information stuck to me from my reading; but more, I must think, from continuous conversation with such friends as Bax and Hyndman and Scheu, and the brisk course of propaganda meetings which were going on at the time, and in which I took my share. Such finish to what of education in practical Socialism as I am capable of I received afterwards from some of my Anarchist friends, from whom I learned, quite against their intention, that Anarchism was impossible, much as I learned from Mill against his intention that Socialism was necessary.

But in this telling how I fell into practical Socialism I have begun, as I perceive, in the middle, for in my position of a well-to-do man, not suffering from the disabilities which oppress a working man at every step, I feel that I might never have been drawn into the practical side of the question if an ideal had not forced me to seek towards it. For politics as politics, i.e., not regarded as a necessary if cumbersome and disgustful means to an end, would never have attracted me, nor when I had become conscious of thewrongs of society as it now is, and the oppression of poor people, could I have ever believed in the possibility of a partial setting right of those wrongs. In other words, I could never have been such a fool as to believe in the happy and "respectable" poor.

If, therefore, my ideal forced me to look for practical Socialism, what was it that forced me to conceive of an ideal? Now, here comes in what I said of my being (in this paper) a type of a certain group of mind.

Before the uprising of modern Socialism almost all intelligent people either were, or professed themselves to be, quite contented with the civilization of this century. Again, almost all of these really were thus contented, and saw nothing to do but to perfect the said civilization by getting rid of a few ridiculous survivals of the barbarous ages. To be short, this was the Whig frame of mind, natural to the modern prosperous middle-class men, who, in fact, as far as mechanical progress is concerned, have nothing to ask for, if only Socialism would leave them alone to enjoy their plentiful style.

But besides these contented ones there were others who were not really contented, but had a vague sentiment of repulsion to the triumph of civilization, but were coerced into silence by the measureless power of Whiggery. Lastly, there were a few who were in open rebellion against the said Whiggery—a few, say two, Carlyle and Ruskin. The latter, before my days of practical Socialism, was my master towards the ideal aforesaid, and, looking backward, I cannot help saying, by the way, how deadly dull the world would have been twenty years ago but for Ruskin! It was through him that I learned to give form to my discontent, which I must say was not by any means vague. Apart from the desire to produce beautiful things, the leading passion of my life has been and is hatred of modern civilization. What shall I say of it now, when the words are put into my mouth, my hope of its destruction—what shall I say of its supplanting by Socialism?

What shall I say concerning its mastery of and its waste of mechanical power, its commonwealth so poor, its enemies of the commonwealth so rich, its stupendous organization—for the misery of life! Its contempt of simple pleasures which everyone could enjoy but for its folly? Its eyeless vulgarity which has destroyed art, the one certain solace of labour? All this I felt then as now, but I did not know why it was so. The hope of the past times was gone, the struggles of mankind for many ages had produced nothing but this sordid, aimless, ugly confusion; the immediate future seemed to me likely to intensify all the present evils by sweeping away the last survivals of the days before the dull squalor of civilization had settled down on the world. This was a bad look-out indeed, and, if I may mention myself as a personality and not as a mere type, especially so to a man of my disposition, careless of metaphysics and religion, as well as of scientific analysis, but with a deep love of the earth and the life on it, and a passion for the history of the past of mankind. Think of it! Was it all to end in a counting-house on the top of a cinder-heap, with Podsnap's drawing-room in the offing, and a Whig committee dealing out champagne to the rich and margarine to the poor in such convenient proportions as would make all men contented together, though the pleasure of the eyes was gone from the world, and the place of Homer was to be taken by Huxley? Yet, believe me, in my heart, when I really forced myself to look towards the future, that is what I saw in it, and, as far as I could tell, scarce anyone seemed to think it worth while to struggle against such a consummation of civilization. So there I was in for a fine pessimistic end of life, if it had not somehow dawned on me that amidst all this filth of civilization the seeds of a great change, what we others call Social-Revolution, were beginning to germinate. The whole face of things was changed to me by that discovery, and all I had to do then in order to become a Socialist was to hook myself on to the practical movement, which, as before said, I have tried to do as well as I could.

To sum up, then the study of history and the love and practice of art forced me into a hatred of the civilization which, if things were to stop as they are, would turn history into inconsequent nonsense, and make art a collection of the curiosities of the past, which would have no serious relation to the life of the present.

But the consciousness of revolution stirring amidst our hateful modern society prevented me, luckier than many others of artistic perceptions, from crystallizing into a mere railer against "progress" on the one hand, and on the other from wasting time and energy in any of the numerous schemes by which the quasi-artistic of the middle classes hope to make art grow when it has no longer any root, and thus I became a practical Socialist.

A last word or two. Perhaps some of our friends will say, what have we to do with these matters of history and art? We want by means of Social-Democracy to win a decent livelihood, we want in some sort to live, and that at once. Surely any one who professes to think that the question of art and cultivation must go before that of the knife and fork (and there are some who do propose that) does not understand what art means, or how that its roots must have a soil of a thriving and unanxious life. Yet it must be remembered that civilization has reduced the workman to such a skinny and pitiful existence, that he scarcely knows how to frame a desire for any life much better than that which he now endures perforce. It is the province of art to set the true ideal of a full and reasonable life before him, a life to which the perception and creation of beauty, the enjoyment of real pleasure that is, shall be felt to be as necessary to man as his daily bread, and that no man, and no set of men, can be deprived of this except by mere opposition, which should be resisted to the utmost.

WILLIAM·MORRIS

Walter Crane

Afterword:
The Communist Poet-Laureate: William Morris's Chants for Socialists *
Nicholas Salmon

I t would be fair to assume that before his entrance into the national political arena Morris had only a limited knowledge of the upsurge in interest in popular music and verse. Yet this was an important element in the resurgence of Victorian working-class culture. As the music critic of the *Times*, Francis Hueffer, remarked in 1877: 'It is no exaggeration to say that with the exception perhaps of natural science... there is no branch of human knowledge, or of hum an art, in which the change that the half-century of the Queen's reign has seen is so marked as it is in the love of music'.[1] Everybody sang: they sang in their homes they sang part songs and glees in groups, they joined choral societies, and they sang in crowds. Most significantly, some of the more enlightened members of the middle classes recognised that songs could be used as a means of mobilising support for campaigns for social reform. Songs began to emerge as essential tools in many of the hard-fought battles for social and moral betterment amongst which can be cited various evangelical crusades, the temperance movement, female emancipation and the fight against poverty. Songs had become, in fact, essential contemporary weapons of propaganda.

Given this background it is not surprising that Morris's first political poem was a song, which dated from the period of his involvement with the Eastern Question Association (EQA). 'Wake,

The Communist Poet-Laureate: William Morris's Chants for Socialists

* First published in *The Journal of William Morris Studies 14.3* (Winter 2001). Nicholas Salmon (1957-2001) edited the *Journal* from 1993 to 1998, and was an enthusiastic member of the William Morris Society. During this period he also edited the *William Morris Library* for Thoemmes Press. The *William Morris Internet Archive* is dedicated to Nick Salmon in appreciation for all the work he did in creating the archive. His early death in 2001 deprived us of an energetic champion of William Morris.

The
Communist
Poet-Laureate:
William
Morris's
Chants for
Socialists

London Lads' was written in January 1878, and
although not the first of Morris's published poems
designed to be sung (the honour of which goes to a
carol 'French Noel: Masters, in this Hall' printed in
1860 in a *Collection of Ancient Christmas Carols*
with an arrangement for four voices by Edmund
Sedding[2]) was his first excursion into poetry
designed primarily for propaganda purposes. The
idea for a song to introduce the large Exeter Hall
meeting of 16 January 1878 called 'to protest
against England being dragged into war'[3] at which
Morris delivered his controversial speech on the
'Opening of the Dardanelles',[4] was, according to
Morris, suggested by Mr. F W Chesson[5]. Written to
the air 'The Hardy Norseman's Home of Yore' – a
refrain returned to later in the *Chants for Socialists*
– it was printed on one side of a single demi-octavo
sheet which was circulated among the predominately
working-class audience before t he meeting.[6]

The reception of 'Wake, London Lads' was
everything that Morris could have desired. The
Exeter Hall meeting attracted a vast audience
sufficient to fill the hall three times over. It was with
great difficulty that the more rowdy members of the
war-party were kept out. The noise in the street was
such, as Morris wrote to his wife Janey three days
later, that it 'was like the sea roaring against a
lighthouse'.[7] A choir and suitable accompaniment
had been organised to perform 'Wake, London
Lads' at the beginning of the proceedings. 'They
sang it well together'. Morris went on to say,
adding:

> ...they struck up while we were just ready to
> come on to the platform & you can imagine I

felt rather excited when I heard them begin to tune up: they stopped at the end of each verse and cheered lustily: we came on to the platform just about the middle of it.[8]

From Morris's remark in the same letter that he h ad a bundle of copies of the song in his possession it is quite possible that it was also sung at other meetings organised by the EQA around the time.

An examination of the text of t he song shows that Morris had already gained a good working knowledge of the requirements of this form of propaganda. Although not entirely free of the archaisms and redundancies that characterise much of his earlier poetry, the language is direct, the diction is clear, and the rhythm ideally suited to the accompaniment. However, despite its simplicity of construction its appeal is unashamedly didactic. Morris bids the 'London Lads' to remember how their forefathers had sacrificed their lives during past moments of England's history – such as the Civil War – in order that 'lovely freedom's glimmering spark' should light up the land.[9] The threat of participation in an 'unjust war' on behalf of the Turks had, he claimed, descended like a metaphorical fog on the land of liberty, and under its cover the forces of reaction threatened to reforge the chains of oppression not only in Europe but also at home. It was the duty of all true Englishmen to cherish their tradition of liberty and, by opposing the forces of reaction, ensure its survival into the future.

Further evidence that Morris was aware of t he power of these songs as a means of mobilising

The
Communist
Poet-Laureate:
William
Morris's
*Chants for
Socialists*

popular support occurred later in the same campaign. A little over a month after t he success of the Exeter Hall meeting the tide of popular opinion had turned sharply in favour of the war party and the EQA found its meetings increasingly disrupted by opponents. On 25 February 1878 the force of this reaction led Morris to write to his daughter May that 'the people are gone crazy, & are quite determined on war if the Government can find any excuse for picking a quarrel'.[10] The reason for this reversal of fortunes was that the Government had been successful in exploiting the patriotic fervour of the working classes. As Morris put it 'people go about in a Rule Britannia style that turn's one's stomach'.[11] Significantly, this patriotism soon found its way into the Music Halls, where shrewd managers were always eager to take advantage of the enthusiasm generated by appeals to national pride. Numerous songs and sketches were written on the theme, one of which was even responsible for adding a new word to the language: 'jingoism'. Ironically, it was a word that was soon to enter Morris's own vocabulary.[12]

The popular success of these Music Hall songs was not lost on Morris. Early in 1880 he used the refrain of one of them – *'Our Country Right or Wrong'* – as the title for a lecture he wrote aimed for delivery to a radical or liberal audience in the run up to the general election of that year.[13] This lecture, in which Morris made his most sustained arrack on the horrors of war, is interesting because it extended and clarified the argument of 'Wake, London Lads' in its condemnation of the sentiment behind such songs:

The
Communist
Poet-Laureate:
William
Morris's
*Chants for
Socialists*

...false patriotism becomes National Vain-glory, which is both begotten of ignorance and begets it: a legacy of the injustice of past times, it breeds injustice in us in the present that we may be unjustly dealt with in the future: it gabbles of the valour of our forefathers, while it is busy in undoing the deeds that their valiant lives accomplished: it prates of the interests of our country, while it is laying the trail of events which will ruin the fortunes, and break the hearts of the citizens.[14]

Later, at the beginning of his active campaign for the socialist cause, he wrote to his daughter Jenny of the intense irritation he experienced when 'two young mashers...hummed and whistled music-hall tunes' during a railway journey to a lecture engagement.[15]

The success of Wake, London Lads led Morris to write a series of songs for the socialist cause. As he wrote in *Commonweal* in April 1885 he was entirely in agreement with John Ruskin that a 'cause which cannot be sung of is not worth following'.[16] The first group of these songs were begun in 1884 when ' The Day is Coming' appeared in Justice on 29th March. The latter was subsequently published by the Democratic Federation as an eight page pamphlet sold for a penny.[17] This was followed by 'The Voice of Toil' (published in *Justice*, 5 April 1884, p5, and later coupled with 'The Day is Coming' and issued as another eight page penny pamphlet), 'All for the Cause' *Justice*, 19 April 1884, p. 5), and 'No Master' *Justice*, 7 June 1884, p. 5).[18] These together with 'The March of the

The
Communist
Poet-Laureate:
William
Morris's
*Chants for
Socialists*

Workers' and 'The Message of the March Wind' which appeared in *Commonweal* in February and March 1885, were subsequently gathered together under the title of *Chants for Socialists* and published by the Socialist League in 1885. Later in the same year another edition was also published which included a further 'chant', 'Down Among the Dead Men', which was the only one of the series not to make a contemporary appearance in either *Justice* or *Commonweal*.

In addition Morris wrote two other songs. The first of these, 'Socialists at Play', appeared in the July 1885 edition of the *Commonweal* and also as a pamphlet published by the Socialist League. Two years later, after Bloody Sunday, 'A Death Song' was issued as a penny pamphlet as a memorial to Alfred Linnell who had died as a result of the injuries he received in Trafalgar Square. This song was included in later editions of *Chants for Socialists*.

These poems were written at a time when Morris, following his experiences with the EQA and the conclusions he had reached in his series of lectures published as *Hopes and Fears for Art* (1882), had begun to reassess his attitude to poetry. This revaluation occurred when he came to the conclusion that the decorative arts were being destroyed by capitalism. As he wrote to Georgiana Burne-Jones on 21 August 1883: 'Poetry goes with the hand-arts I think, and like them has now become unreal: the arts have got to die, what is left of them, before they can be born again'.[19] In another letter to Georgiana Burne-Jones he went further and implicitly criticised the creative motivation of his own early poetry, saying that he had no sympathy with Swinburne's

The
Communist
Poet-Laureate:
William
Morris's
*Chants for
Socialists*

Tristram of Lyonesse because it was founded on an 'intense study and love of literature' which entirely ignored the requirements of an age in which 'the surroundings of life are so stern and unplayful, that nothing can take serious hold of people, or should do so, but that which is rooted deepest in reality'.[20] It was to be a not altogether successful attempt to create such a poetry of revolutionary realism which was to occupy him during his first few years with the Social Democratic Federation and the Socialist League.

Morris was challenging literary opinion in suggesting that it was the role of the poet in the nineteenth century to confront reality rather than use his or her art as a means of escape. Many of his contemporaries were appalled to see him abandon what they saw as his true vocation. Edward Burne-Jones, in a letter to an unidentified correspondent written soon after Morris started his propaganda work for 'the Cause', stated:

I shall never try again to leave the world than I can control to my heart's desire – the little world that has the walls of my workroom for its furtherest horizon – and I want Morris back to it, and want him to write divine books and leave the rest.[21]

George Gissing was just as emphatic. Having heard that Morris had been charged with disorderly conduct and striking a policeman at a trial of eight socialists who bad been held for obstruction in September 1885, he wrote sadly to his brother:

... what the devil is such a man doing in that gallery? It is painful to me beyond expression. Why cannot he write poetry in the shade? ... Keep apart, keep apart, and preserve one's soul

73

The
Communist
Poet-Laureate:
William
Morris's
*Chants for
Socialists*

alive – that is the teaching for the day. It is ill to have been born in these times, but one can make a world within the world.[22]

Even so Morris appears to have been reluctant at first to assume the poet laureateship of the socialist movement. He even approached Swinburne on 17 November 1883 with the suggestion that the latter join the Democratic Federation and contribute some verse to one of the early editions of *Justice*: 'You ought to write us a song, you know, that's what you ought to do: I mean to be set to music, for singing at meetings of the faithful'.[23] Despite politely claiming a certain sympathy with Morris's political views Swinburne – probably aware of his own poetic reputation – discreetly declined the invitation:

I do trust you will not...regard me as a dilettante democrat if I say that I would rather not join any Federation. What good I can do to the cause...will I think be done as well or better from an independent point of action and of view.[24]

The chants themselves reveal that Morris had internalised at least one of the lessons he had learned from his participation in the EQA. To achieve the maximum propaganda value Morris wrote the songs for occasions when strong emotions were likely to be aroused. Many of the chants were thus written specifically for important events such as Hyndman's debate with Bradlaugh on 17 April 1884, an entertainment of the Socialist League held at the South Place Institute on 11 June 1885 and for Alfred Linnell's funeral on 18 November 1887. For the latter occasion Morris wrote 'A Death Song' which was sold as a penny pamphlet with an illustration by Walter Crane depicting a policeman clubbing the unfortunate Linnell.[25] All proceeds from the sale of this pamphlet were donated to a fund for the benefit of Linnell's orphans.

To ensure the chants were immediately accessible to working-class audiences they were designed to be sung to well-known refrains. The two most popular were 'The Hardy Norseman's Home of Yore' (used for 'Wake, London Lads' and 'No Master') and 'John Brown's Body lies a Mouldering in the Grave' (used for 'The March of the Workers'). According to May Morris the measure of the latter turned out to be too heavy for the familiar wording of the song. In the Collected Works she explained that this happened because

> ...someone unluckily furnished my father not with the original words as a guide, but with another set of verses, the long racing metre of which he followed. When he found out how much simpler the original John Brown song was, he was rather vexed about it.[26]

It is possible that Morris was actually presented with the words of the 'Battle Hymn of the Republic'.

The problem to be confronted when considering the success of the *Chants* is one of critical perspective. This arises because Morris decided to include many of them in *Poems by the Way* (1891) and therefore offer them up for critical appraisal. Why he did this is not clear. Mackail has pointed out that a vast amount of previously unpublished material was left out of this volume. This included a number of longer narrative poems which dated from the period of *The Earthly Paradise*. If Morris had decided to include these they would certainly have received sympathetic attention from the critics.

The
Communist
Poet-Laureate:
William
Morris's
*Chants for
Socialists*

Even leaving these aside, Mackail went on to state 'there are still sufficient on these yet unpublished pieces, – lyrics, sonnets, and ballads – to make up a second volume of 'Poems by the Way' as large as the first'.[27] Given the extent of this unpublished material, the fact that the volume was compiled in association with the sober Fairfax Murray, and the knowledge that Morris had no illusions about the poetic value of the chants, there must have been a reason why he chose to have them reprinted.

Part of the explanation for their inclusion probably lies in the title of the volume itself: *Poems by the Way*. It included material which ranged from ballads, love-lyrics and romances from the period of *The Earthly Paradise*, through Nordic translations and verses produced for various pictures, tapestries and embroideries, to the later medievalist romances such as 'Goldilocks and Goldilocks'. As each of these groups represented a stage in his poetic development, to exclude any reference to the socialist verses would have undoubtedly been regarded by Morris as hypocritical.

It is also possible that he wanted to make a more specific statement by their inclusion. In the early 1890s various critics began to consider the possible successors to Tennyson as poet-laureate. At this time Morris was still regarded as one of the main contenders. As one critic put it 'a formidable competitor for any one save Lord Tennyson himself'.[28] What the critics objected to, however, was the fact that Morris had deserted poetry for socialism. Poems by the Way was inevitably going to be the volume on which his future reputation was to rest, and it may have been this thought that made him decide to include the socialist verses as a reminder of his continued commitment to 'the Cause'.

The first edition of *Poems by the Way* issued by the Kelmscott Press in 1891, was limited to a mere 250 copies sold at two guineas each,[29] and was almost completely passed over by the critics. Indeed, the half dozen reviews that did appear mostly followed the publication of the cheaper Chiswick Press edition which was published later in the same year.[30] The socialist poetry evoked from these contemporary reviewers one of two responses: either it was completely ignored or viewed simply as the inferior product of a once great poet whose Muse had sadly deserted him following his conversion to socialism. Of the latter the following remarks are representative: an anonymous reviewer in the *Saturday Review* complained of Morris's 'almost pathetically crude Socialism'.[31] Richard Garnett in the *Illustrated London News* that there was 'but little poetic worth to Mr. Morris's purely socialistic poetry',[32] and Oliver Elton writing in the *Academy*, after showing himself to be the most sympathetic to Morris's political standpoint, concluding sadly that 'the songs... which are written expressly in honour of the "Cause" are not always the happiest or strongest in the book'.[33]

Judgements such as these – although fair in literary terms – have had the effect of greatly underestimating the impact of the Chants as socialist propaganda.[34] They were immensely popular amongst the rank and file of the movement. According to Buxton Forman the *Chants* ran to two editions in 1885, another in 1888 (when they were coupled with 'The Socialist Platform' and the

The
Communist
Poet-Laureate:
William
Morris's
*Chants for
Socialists*

'Manifesto of the Socialist League') and one more in 1892 (similar to the second edition of 1885).[35] May Morris confirms that there was always 'a steady demand at meetings and open-air demonstrations' for copies of the penny pamphlets.[36] Christopher Waters has pointed out that the *Chants* also figured prominently in wider collections of socialist songs. A number of them were published in Carpenter's *Chants for Labour: A Song-Book of the People* (1888)[37] and thereafter they were included in no less than eight further collections which appeared between 1888 and 1912.[38] According to Waters, of the 532 titles featured in these nine songbooks no less than eight per cent were written by Morris.[39]

The *Chants* had a far wider appeal than Morris could have envisaged. Shortly after the publication of 'The Day is Coming' in September 1883, for example, the Christian Socialist announced that the poem 'was read from the pulpit of at least one London church on 22nd September, and will be heard from other pulpits during the next two weeks'.[40] The same paper also urged its readers to purchase a copy of the song as 'it ought to stir the blood of any Englishman that hears it'.[41] The *Chants* even reached the United States where they were taken up by bodies such as the Women's Socialist Union and the Knights of Labour. Many of them were also published in radical and socialist newspapers such as *The Appeal to Reason*, *The Coming Nation*, the *Workmen's Advocate* and *People*.[42]

Their main purpose was, of course, to enliven meetings and entertainments of the SDF and SL, and to act as a counter to the activities of the various other organisations seeking to attract working class support. In this respect they were again remarkably successful. When a large open-air meeting was held in Norwich Market Place on 12 August 1888, for example, Morris's chant 'No Master' was sung by the assembled crowd in opposition to no less than two Salvation Army bands, a Gospel Band and the peals of the nearby St. Peter Mancroft's Church.43 An anonymous 'Platform Guest', writing in the Norfolk Daily Standard, reported that 'the audience sang with gusto'.[44]

The *Chants* also served as entertainments on socialist outings. E P Thompson quotes the Bradford socialist F W Jowett recalling how he and his comrades sang 'The March of the Workers' with enthusiasm on walks in the surrounding countryside, all the time believing that the people were indeed 'marching on'.[45] Morris, himself, volunteered to take the responsibility for funding a Democratic Federation band in order to provide accompaniment for the songs,[46] while later, no less a person than Gustav Holst formed a choir which met at Kelmscott House to sing the *Chants* at meetings of the Hammersmith Branch of the Socialist League.[47]

The popular success of the *Chants* shows that Morris had made considerable advances in his appreciation of the essential requirements of a popular song. The basic weakness of 'Wake, London Lads' had been that Morris's bourgeois paternalism had expressed itself in a moral appeal to the working classes more suitable to be read than sung. Most popular late Victorian songs, however, had little intellectual content to distract the singer

79

The
Communist
Poet-Laureate:
William
Morris's
*Chants for
Socialists*

but instead concentrated on reinforcing shared sentiments through simplicity of construction. To be successful they needed to he easy to memorise and to be in tune with the ideas expressed in the lyrics. The sonorous language and rousing choruses of the *Chants* were an entirely appropriate complement to their dominant theme of the workers marching inexorably to the rebirth of society. In this sense at least, Morris can be seen responding to the realities of his age and exploiting an existing form for his own political ends.

However, borrowed forms impose their own limitations. By exploiting the sentiment to be gained from black and white judgements, simple antitheses and banal generalisations, the Chants lay themselves open to the criticism that they romanticise both the cause and the workers. As E P Thompson has pointed out, white the *Chants* are both moving and effective as propaganda they 'cannot be said to lay the foundations of a poetry of "revolutionary socialism"'.[48] More recently Jack Mitchell has extended this criticism by arguing that Morris failed to portray the reality of ordinary people engaged in the historic class struggles of their era, primaiily because he was incapable of escaping the traditional conventions which required the poet to focus on the dreams of a 'sensitive individual psyche'.[49]

There is much truth in Mitchel's argument. The *Chants* are full of the optimism characteristic of Morris's early years in the socialist movement, and there can be no mistaking the personal nature of the utopia he envisaged for the future.[50] In 'The Day is Coming', the first of the *Chants*, it is 'the wonderful days a-coming, when all shall be better than well'[51]

80

which provides the antithetical structure in which the positive future is contrasted with the negative present. The resulting utopia includes all the usual Morrisian features: good housing; enjoyable work; leisure, food; fellowship; a beautiful environment; and, of course, a share in art. However, precisely because this utopia is individual and abstract its contrast with capitalism exaggerates the latter's vices to such an extent that it loses contact with reality altogether. If one took 'The Day is Coming' as a realistic presentation of working-class conditions in the nineteenth century, it would be necessary to accept that all the workers were lodged like 'swine', 'too faint and weary to stand', fearful of 'the hunger-wolf anear' and liable at any moment to 'droop and die'. One can't help feeling that mobilising such a band of miserable people is a forlorn hope.

A similar problem is encountered when one considers Morris's portrayal of the working class. As has already been remarked, the *Chants* were primarily written to be sung at meetings of the SDF and SL. Yet on close examination it can be seen that they were all directed at the enlightened working men who were already committed to 'the Cause'. Clearly Morris felt it was important to encourage such converts, and the *Chants* are full of appeals to these 'few against the world'[52] as they are styled in 'No Master', to accept the moral responsibility for the education of the mass of their brothers so that the revolutionary transformation of society can be accomplished. Unfortunately, in emphasising the value of this work Morris sacrifices the remainder of the labouring population to a Blakean wilderness. 'How long shall they reproach us', he asks in 'The

The
Communist
Poet-Laureate:
William
Morris's
*Chants for
Socialists*

Day is Coming', 'where crowd on crowd they dwell, / Poor ghosts of the wicked city, the gold-crushed hungry hell?'[53] In no way can this be termed the language of social realism.[54]

It is difficult to imagine the Chants being sung today. Now we have spindoctors, cliché-mongers and design consultants. Attempts to get the attention of the working-class are now firmly in the hands of the media. Yet, despite their obvious limitations, the Chants show Morris responding to contemporary society in a way that disproves the absurd allegations that he was some sort of romantic dreamer out of touch with his age. Morris, without doubt, was the first Victorian modernist.

Notes

The
Communist
Poet-Laureate:
William
Morris's
*Chants for
Socialists*

1 Quoted in the introduction to *The Parlour Song Book*, ed. Michael R Turner, (London: Michael Joseph, 1972), p. 2.

2 'French Noel: Masters, in the Hall' was written while Morris was working in the office of the architect, Edmund Street, presumably under the persuasion of his fellow pupils who at that time had a taste for part-song. See *The Work of William Morris: An Exhibition Arranged by the William Morris Society*, (London: William Morris Society, 1962), p. 53.

3 *The Times*, 17 January 1878, p. 6.

4 Eugene D. Lemire, ed., *The Unpublished Lectures of William Morris*, (Detroit: Wayne State University Press, 1969), p. 235. *The Times*, 17 January 1878, p6, carried a report of this speech which may correspond to a MSS on the same subject at the Emery Walker House in Hammersmith.

5 Norman Kelvin, ed., *The Collected Letters of William Morris*, (Princeton: Princeton University Press, 1984), I, pp. 434-36.

6 H. Buxton Forman, *The Books of William Morris: With some Account of his Doings in Literature and in the Allied Arts*, (London, 1897), p. 93.

7 *The Collected Letters of William Morris*, Volume I, pp. 434-36.

8 ibid, I, pp. 434-36.

9 For some inexplicable reason 'Wake, London, Lads' was omitted from the Collected Works, a fact which probably explains why the poem has attracted little critical attention. However, Norman Kelvin has reproduced it in full in *The Collected Letters*, I, pp. 436-37.

10 ibid, I, p. 451.

11 ibid, I, p. 446.

12 See, for example, *The Collected Letters of William Morris*, II(a), pp. 202-04.

13 B.M. Add. MS. 45334[4]. Parts of this lecture were also reprinted under the title 'War and Peace' by May Morris in *William Morris: Artist, Writer Socialist*, (Oxford: Basil Blackwell, 1936), II, pp. 53-62.

83

The
Communist
Poet-Laureate:
William
Morris's
*Chants for
Socialists*

14 B.M. Add, M$.45334[4].

15 *The Collected Letters of William Morris*, II(a), p. 188.

16 *Commonweal*, April 1885, p. 23.

17 *Justice*, 29 March 1884, p. 4.

18 See *The Books of William Morris*, pp. 109-29.

19 *The Collected Letters of William Morris*, II(a), p. 217.

20 ibid, 2,p. 119.

21 Georgiana Burne-Jones, *Memorials of Edward Burne-Jones*, (London, 1906), II, p. 98.

22 Algernon and Ellen Gissing, eds, *Letters of George Gissing to Members of His Family*, (Boston, 1927), pp. 170 and 174.

23 *The Collected Letters of William Morris*, II(a), p. 246.

24 B.M. Add. MS. 45345.

25 *The Books of William Morris*, pp. 128-31.

26 May Morris, ed., *The Collected Works of William Morris*, 24 vols., (London: Longman Green & Co., 1910-15), XXIV, p. xxxiii.

27 John W. Mackail, *The Life of William Morris*, 2 vols., (London: Longmans, 1899), II, p. 257.

28 *Fortnightly Review,* 1 May 1890.

29 *The Books of William Morris*, p. 158.

30 Delbert R. Gardner, *An 'Idle Singer' and His Audience: A Study of William Morris's Poetic Reputation in England, 1858-1900* (The Hague/Paris: Mouton, 1975), p. 91.

31 *Saturday Review*, 6 February 1892.

32 *Illustrated London News*, 9 January 1892, p. 50.

33 *Academy*, February 1892, p. 197.

34 This attitude has continued to the present day. See, for example, J. M. S. Tompkins's *William Morris: An Approach to the Poetry* (London: Cecil Woolf , 1988), in which there is not a single reference to *Chants for Socialists*.

35 *The Books of William Morris*, pp. 118-19 and p. 133.

36 *The Collected Works of William Morris*, XXIV, p. xxxii.

37 See *An 'Idle Singer' and His Audience,* pp. 95-96. Oscar Wilde, in a review of Carpenter's *Chants for Labour* published in the *Pall Mall Gazette* on 15 February 1889, agreed that Morris's contributions had little literary value,

but made the important point that this was because they were designed to be sung rather than read.

38 Chris Waters, 'Morris's "Chants" and the Problems of Socialist Culture', in *Socialism and the Literary Artistry of William Morris*, eds. Florence Boos and Carole Silver (Colombia: University of Missouri Press, 1990), pp. 132-33.

39 ibid, p. 133.

40 Quoted by Jack Lindsay in *William Morris: His Life and Work* (London: Constable, 1975), p. 262.

41 *Christian Socialist*, October 1883, p. 66.

42 See 'Morris's *"Chants" and the Problems of Socialist Culture*', p. 142.

43 *Eastern Daily Press*, 13 August 1888, p. 5.

44 The *Norfolk Daily Standard*, 13 August 1888, p. 3. The Tory paper, *The Norfolk Chronicle and Norwich Gazette* (18 August 1888, p. 3), was, however, less enthusiastic describing the 'chant' as sung 'to a dismal, soul racking tune'.

45 E P Thompson, *William Morris: Romantic to Revolutionary* (London: Merlin Press, 1977), p. 667.

46 'Music for the People', *Justice*, 24 May 1884, p. 1.

47 *The Work of William Morris: An Exhibition Arranged by the William Morris Society*, p. 53.

48 *William Morris: Romantic to Revolutionary*, p. 669.

49 Jack Mitchell, 'William Morris's Aesthetic Relationship to the Contemporary Working Class', *Zeitschrift fur Anglistik und Amerikanistik*, 33: 2 (1985), pp. 153-60.

50 For some comments on the optimistic nature of the Chants see Peter Faulkner's 'Morris's Political Poetry', Ex. Cat., *William Morris Today* (London: ICA, 1984) pp. 34-37.

51 *The Collected Works of William Morris*, IX, p. 180.

52 ibid, IX, pp. 180-81.

53 ibid, XXIV, p. 409.

54 ibid, IX, p. 181.

ALSO FROM REDWORDS

Crossing the 'river of fire' : the socialism of William Morris

by Hassan Mahamdallie

William Morris designed wallpaper; along with furniture, ceramics, stained-glass windows, tapestries, and carpets. He was a painter, he wrote novels, poetry, and translated Icelandic sagas, he wrote on politics, architecture, and the state of art under a growing industrial capitalism and what possibilities existed for life in the future. The ravages of industrial capitalism, imperialism and war, the destruction of the environment, and above all, the enslavement of human labour to the machine appalled him.

As the nineteenth century progressed he become more political and took a giant step across the 'river of fire' and became a revolutionary socialist. Hassan Mahamdallie shows that the socialism of Morris grew out of his view of the past and his hatred for a system of 'shoddy' production and that during the last decades of his life he threw all his energy into the struggle to change the world.

ISBN: 978 1909026 04 9
£9.99

1 Bloomsbury Street, London WC1B 3QE

www.redwords.org.uk

Also available from Bookmarks the **socialist bookshop**

The Point is to Change It!
An introduction to Marxist philosophy
by John Molyneux
£7

A new generation of activists is looking to Marx for answers to the crisis, but a century of Stalinism, academic Marxism and post-Marxism has obscured Marx's philosophy and made it seem inaccessible. In this lively and practical book John Molyneux introduces the framework and key concepts of Marxist philosophy, such as the dialectic and historical materialism.

Using current real world examples throughout, he illustrates the relevance of Marxism for trade unionists, activists and anyone who wants to change the world today.

Defending Multiculturalism: A Guide for the Movement
Edited by Hassan Mahamdallie
£8

This vibrant, hard-hitting and informative collection of essays sets out to defend Britain's multicultural way of life. The contributors challenge David Cameron and others' assertions that multiculturalism is to blame for dividing society.

Contributors include Peter Hain MP, Professor Tariq Modood, Liz Fekete, Professor Danny Dorling, Salma Yaqoob, Ken Livingstone, Edie Friedman, Sabby Dhalu, Martin Smith, Billy Hayes, Weyman Bennett and Dilowar Khan. Poetry by Michael Rosen, Zita Holbourne, Benjamin Zephaniah and Avaes Mohammed, photos by Rehan Jamil.

Bookmarks bookshop,
1 Bloomsbury Street, London WC1B 3QE
020 7637 1848 enquiries@bookmarks.uk.com

www.bookmarksbookshop.co.uk